Where Are the Animals?

Look, and You Will Find Them.

Brenda Kay

Balboa Press books may be ordered through booksellers or by contacting:

Balboa Press
A Division of Hay House
1663 Liberty Drive
Bloomington, IN 47403
www.balboapress.com
1 (877) 407-4847

ISBN: 978-1-5043-0875-5 (sc)
978-1-5043-0876-2 (e)

Print information available on the last page.

Balboa Press rev. date: 06/20/2017

BALBOA.
PRESS
A DIVISION OF HAY HOUSE

Dedicated to my son Steven.

Where are the animals?

Look, and you will find them.

Can you find a magpie in the grass, a kookaburra in the tree?

Here's a plover sitting on its nest.

How many parrots can you see?

Look. See the meat ants on their gravel mound?

The magpie's found something, what could it be?

There's an eagle flying high in the sky, and below it are crows cawing as they fly, ark, ark, ark.

Where are the animals?

The sky grows darker.

A kingfisher returns to its nest, as the flying foxes come out for the night.

A dingo stands on top of the hill, watching as two wallabies hop past.

There are ducks on the dam, some fly away to their homes.

How many can you see?

Where are the animals?

Night is here.

The mopokes call, mo-poke, mo-poke.
Can you see them in the trees?

The dingo howls, aaawwwoooohoooooo.

Look, a full moon rising over the trees.

Do you think there could be something in them?

It's a possum with four eyes!

Aah, it's a mum and her baby.

Where are the animals?

Look, and you will find them.

Activity.

Sit still for a moment.

Look. Listen.

What animals can you see?

Activity.

Sit still for a moment.

Look. Listen.

Can you hear any animal sounds?

Activity.

Stop. Look. Listen. Watch.
Add more animals to these pages as
you find them.

www.ingramcontent.com/pod-product-compliance
Lightning Source LLC
Chambersburg PA
CBHW041132280526
45792CB00013B/2401